Hard Times and Fine Lines

Hard Times and Fine Lines

Israel Mason

Copyright © 2018 by Israel Mason
All rights reserved. This book or any portion thereof
may not be reproduced or used in any manner whatsoever
without the express written permission of the publisher
except for the use of brief quotations in a book review.

Printed in the United States of America

First Printing, 2018

ISBN 978-1-387-86650-2

Lulu Publishing
627 Davis Dr #300
Morrisville, NC 27560
www.lulu.com

To the one who started all this,

and to those who helped me get through it.

Contents

27 May 2015	1
Stand	2
A Grandmother's Advice	3
10 Ways of Looking at an Apple	4
Reflection	7
Return to Innocence	8
Change	10
Regrets	11
Within	12
Flight	13
Sea	14
Winter	15
The Course	16
Visions	17
Wings of Blue	18
Fruit	19
Unlovable	21
Choices	23

If Trees Were Alive	24
The Birds	25
Stay	26
Sincerely, Depression	27
One Away	28
Beauty Within the Beast	29
Goodbye	31
Lie to Me	32
save me	33
Ode to Rain	34
Good Old Peter	35
Who Am I?	37
Colors	39

27 May 2015

I. When I look at the stars,

   I imagine I am looking into your eyes.

   I imagine that you are the Universe,

   And I am your heart.

II. I look at my hands,

   What have I done?

   I look down at you,

   And then at the gun.

III. Hungry cat.

   Mouse.

   Still hungry cat.

   Mouse.

   "I'm a vegetarian."

Stand

25 June 2015

Stand up for what is right,
Stand up and fight the fight.
Whether it be with your body or brain,
Whether it comes like the sun or the rain.
And if you lose you won't feel the shame,
Do it this once and you'll never be the same.
You'll burn with the brightest flame.

Leave your fears behind,
Be whisked away before you're out of time.
Don't trust everyone you meet,
They might try and knock you off your feet.
Be yourself and don't give in.
If you do you'll come to an end.
Be a believer in yourself.

A Grandmother's Advice

22 January 2016

Soon my darling, Soon you'll see,

That Sugar don't always come with Tea.

Soon my darling, Soon you'll know,

Just 'cause it's White, don't mean it's Snow.

Soon my darling, Soon you'll hear,

That the Roads ahead ain't always Clear.

Soon my darling, Soon you'll feel,

That some Wounds don't ever Heal.

Soon my darling, soon you'll realize,

That not Everybody got the same Eyes.

Soon my darling, Soon you'll learn,

Some Things in life just got to be Earned.

Soon my darling, Soon you'll fear,

The Predators, that don't just hunt Deer.

Soon my darling, Soon you'll be,

All Alone, without advice from Me.

So Remember what I Say,

'Cause you're gonna Use it one of these Days.

10 Ways of Looking at an Apple

2 February 2017

I

A red skin,

Protecting a white flesh.

A hardened heart,

Protecting its innocence.

II

Five points,

Five like a star.

One with the Universe,

One with my Heart.

III

A living thing,

Until plucked from its tree.

An Apple, I guess,

Is just like me.

IV

The rumored forbidden fruit,

Stolen from its youth.

It cannot have its own tree…

Someone has stolen the seeds.

V

An Apple is a Flower,

An Apple is a Tree.

An Apple is everything,

But it is not Free.

VI

A Tiny world,

With a sheltering Atmosphere,

Until it is shattered…

There is no cure for disaster.

VII

Red, white, a bit of green,

Just like Christmas,

Except in the Spring.

VIII

A sweet flesh,

Hides a bitter center.

Like a sweet smile,

Hides an inner sinner.

IX

With a tender, soft texture,

An apple gets bruised.

Now no one wants it,

But did it ask to be abused?

X

An Apple is a teardrop,

From a lonely tree,

Saddened because what once was,

No longer will be.

Reflection

14 February 2017

I remember when, way back then,

I could look at the sunset,

And find beauty there- in.

I remember the line where two worlds met,

A world for the birds that fly in the sky,

And a world for man and beasts of the land.

Where the breeze announces its presence with a warm tender sigh,

And the gentle sea washes over the sand.

I remember being mesmerized by the way the leaves fell,

And the way the wind blew.

Entranced with the swirly patterns in a shell,

My young eyes infatuated with things anew.

And even now, I remember the day,

My sweet child-like innocence faded away.

Return to Innocence

14 February 2017

Do you remember how,

When you were little,

The smallest things provoked a smile,

Like the cat running away with the fiddle?

The ants on the tree,

Warranted your undivided attention,

And the birds in the sky,

Were your hopes and dreams extended.

The rocks on the ground were beautiful,

The clouds were dragons and butterflies,

The curiosity inside you plentiful,

As endless and wide as the skies.

But eventually, things didn't stand out like they used to,

The beauty in simplicity was gone.

Your walks down the road were rushed through,

And you wore glasses to block the sun.

You hardly noticed the moving trees,

And you forgot the secrets of the wind.

You slept as you flew across boundless seas,

And the world around you was no longer yours to defend.

You resented the songs of the morning sparrows,

And you cut down the tree that scratched against your window.

Your mind had become dull and narrow,

And you cried bitter tears into your pillow.

The older you got, the sadder you grew.

You could no longer see the beauty in the surrounding world,

And the many precious moments you had became few.

When you lost all you had, and you wanted to curl,

In someone's arms, and be comforted,

And no one was there,

You cared less about the treasure you had hoarded,

And more about what nature had to share.

So as you stared out of the window into the rain,

You noticed how the wind blew it sideways,

How beautiful were the drops on the pane,

And the trees became a maze.

You noticed how the air that filled your lungs as a child,

Was no longer as satisfying.

You allowed your senses to run wild,

As you lay there dying.

The return to innocence is truly this.

Change

31 August 2017

The sacred whisper of leaves of green,

The quiet hum of a crystal stream.

The distant call of a mourning dove,

The cotton clouds in the skies above.

The memories I hold deep within,

The visions seen when I dream of Then.

Oh, how I wish I could return,

To that Time before the seasons turned.

Before the summer turned to fall,

Before the day I lost it all.

Regrets

1 September 2017

Cold, pale fingers in my hand,

A breathless body in my lap.

I tried to race against the sand,

But the sandman forgot his cap.

I lie down at night and think of You,

How You loved to watch the butterflies,

How You loved to climb to see the view,

How the Stars would dance within Your Eyes.

If I could wish You back to me I would,

I'd hold You close one more time.

I'd have done everything I could,

To make sure I noticed all the signs.

I would have noticed Your happiness dwindle,

I would have seen the twinkle leave Your eye.

I would have looked above for a miracle,

So I wouldn't have to watch You die.

Within

27 September 2017

The wind blows the trees,

The flowers lure the bees.

The sun shines on the dew drops,

The snow falls on the mountain tops.

The deer drink from the glistening stream,

The wings of butterflies shimmer and gleam.

The sparrow sings its lovely song,

My heart tells me this is where I belong.

Here in the Forest of my dreams,

Here where everything is as it seems.

Here with the fairies that dance with light,

Here with majestic swans in glorious flight.

Here in the clearing where my knight awaits,

Here, left only to the desires of fate.

Here within these golden walls,

Here, where my heart calls.

Here where there are always secrets to find,

Here, within the shadows of my mind.

Flight

3 October 2017

The blinds block what you might see,

The closed doors protect you from who might arrive.

The lights keep the shadows hidden away,

The restraints are what keep you alive.

You close your eyes,

Steady your breath,

Clench your fists,

And push away your desire for death.

The doctor comes,

Turns off the lights,

And opens the blinds.

You start to forget your fear of heights.

The shadows come in waves,

The people pass in herds.

The window shows you what you feared you would see

Your mind's eye of what you deserve.

The doctor comes back,

Turns on the lights,

And closes the blinds.

With him, he brings the night,

And with it, comes your majestic flight.

Sea

3 October 2017

Homlier than Home,

Lovelier than Love,

More than Most,

Covering the Coast,

My Sea.

Winter

5 October 2017

Blackbirds stark against the snow,

Bare trees reach toward the sky.

The Arctic Fox watches the crow,

The mice scamper down below.

Footsteps mark the white landscape,

Lost voices travel with the wind.

The mountains stand to greet the day,

Ghosts of the past come out to play.

Water moves beneath the ice,

Shadows run within the breeze.

Camouflaged creatures duck and hide,

Everything else tries to survive.

Suddenly everything goes still.

They have heard me.

They know I am here.

The Course

7 October 2017

The sun shines,

The wind cries.

The snow falls,

The crow calls.

A man runs,

A man follows.

A man shoots,

A man falls.

The blood stains,

The snow red.

A man goes,

The other dead.

The sun shines,

The wind cries.

The snow falls,

The crow calls.

All is well…

Visions

8 October 2017

The World is quiet.

The landscape is blank.

The people are gone.

The wind is silent.

The waters are still.

The birds do not sing.

The clouds do not move.

Nothing is alive.

I am all alone.

And it is all my fault.

That the World is dead.

Fire burns in my eyes.

Blood runs down my face.

But I could not stop,

Once I had started.

So the World is dead,

At least in my Head.

Wings of Blue

10 October 2017

The last breath that she drew,

Brought with it Wings of Blue.

A quiet flutter-- gone.

From the window it flew,

Into the shining Sun.

It carried with it Dreams,

And memories of Time.

It traveled through the Trees,

With Trunks made of laughter,

And Branches made of love.

It also carried Tears,

And deeply hidden Fears.

Visions seen in Darkness,

Reflections in Mirrors,

And overwhelming Sadness.

Across the Oceans deep,

Alongside the Shadows.

Traveling through her Life,

Through good Times and bad Times.

Through Happiness and Strife,

Until finally Ending,

At the very Beginning.

Fruit

7 November 2017

I walked with the detective,

He showed me the crime scene.

He asked me what I saw.

I said, "A fruit basket,

A cabinet and a sofa."

"Now look closer," he said.

"I don't see anything else."

"Notice," he told me.

So I looked really hard.

And it seemed as if the cabinet,

Had a fresh coat of paint.

"It's been painted," I told him.

Then he walked over to the cabinet,

And peeled it off. The paint, I mean.

There was purple underneath.

"Now what does this make you think of?" he asked.

"Prince."

He chuckled. "Besides that."

"I don't know… Grapes."

"Right." he said. Then he walked to the fruit basket.

"Is this a grape?" he asked.

"No. It's a plum." I also went to the fruit basket.

"Now eat it." he said, holding out the fruit to me.

I took the fruit. "It tastes like a grape!" I exclaimed.

"Doesn't it? Now eat one of these."

He held out grapes to me.

I took the grapes. "These taste like plums!"

"Don't they?" he said.

"Isn't it amazing how a fruit can look like itself,

And taste like another?

Or look like another,

And taste like itself?" he asked.

Unlovable

4 December 2017

"I am unlovable" you told me,

So I sought out to prove you wrong.

I did my best to set you free,

I did my best, I tried for so long.

"Love is a fool's game," you said,

"It's a waste of time."

"I'd rather see myself dead,

Than let you believe those lies,"

I replied.

I gave you flowers,

And all of me.

You took all of my power,

And laughed gleefully.

Still I would not give up on you.

I tried to win you over with dinners.

I worked so hard to push through,

But your impassable walls never got thinner.

I told you how I felt,

About love being a two-way thing.

And you said, "That's how the cards were dealt."

It was then that I had truly seen,

That you were never going to love me.

So I left you, Happy and smiling,

While I was left Broken and crying.

Whatever had hurt you,

Was now hurting me.

And my heart-

It grew back crookedly.

So you left your mark on me…

The pain you kept so well hidden,

Is now mine to bear.

And now I understand,

How it feels,

To truly be…

Unlovable.

Choices

14 December 2017

If I'd had the choice,

I would have said no.

But the choice was made for me,

And I had no say so.

If I had the choice now,

I would still say no.

I don't deserve what's happened,

But there's no way to make it go.

I can't see without seeing,

I can't feel without feeling.

I can't love without loving,

I can't live without reliving,

Every moment I spent with you.

If Trees Were Alive

14 December 2017

If trees were alive,

With human souls and eyes,

Would it hurt more when we cut them down?

Or would we grow cold and distant,

From the genocide our wants and needs prescribe?

I'm not convinced though,

That we wouldn't.

Because there are people with human souls and eyes,

Who die at the hands of those who don't.

The Birds

14 December 2017

Listen.

Do you hear them?

The Birds?

They call for you.

They want you to join them.

In the sky.

But the only way to get there is if you…

Let go, and fly.

Stay

14 December 2017

Hold my hand,

Guide me home.

Stay as long as you can,

I can't do this alone.

You are my sanity,

My only reprieve.

In you I see my vanity,

Please. Don't ever leave.

Sincerely, Depression

19 December 2017

If my happiness only comes in blurs of Amber and white,

Should I leave this pathetic life of desire behind me?

This life filled with heartache and betrayal,

This life of charity ignored by its many suitors.

If I left this pathetic life behind me,

Who's to say it would be better.

I believe I am destined for pain.

It is the only way to treat someone like me.

Someone who has broken the hearts of many,

Someone who has even broken my own heart.

I would not give myself the satisfaction,

Of finally being freed from my prison.

This prison of feelings and emotions.

I've tried, but only been left with bloody scratches on the walls.

I've tried, but I can't bring myself to fall so far.

Because even though I don't deserve to be caught,

I won't be able to face jumping without knowing,

That reassuring arms will be there to catch me,

And release me back to myself.

One Away

28 December 2017

I'm one smile away from falling apart,

One hug away from a broken heart.

One glance away from losing it all,

One step away from taking the fall.

One glare away from fighting myself,

One word away from learning nothing's left.

One minute away from facing the end,

And one heartbeat away from losing my friend.

Beauty Within the Beast
30 December 2017

Hard, Black scales cover my face
Cold, dark eyes gaze into space
Long, sharp talons reach for cold
Warm, bright heart turned to stone
Hidden in shadows, left alone.

Look into my darkened eyes.
Can you see how it cries?
My soul still fighting for itself
For how it was before I left.
I used to be able to see me
Reflected so true, so purely
Within my features, my smile.
But now that is long gone

Can you save me?
Can my past come to be?
Or is it too late
Consumed by rage and hate.
Am I no longer there?
Am I just an empty stare.
Please try to see it

A small flicker, dimly lit

I need you to.

I no longer will do.

Search deep, deeper than me,

To, within the beast, find beauty

Goodbye

1 January 2018

With this toast, I say goodbye.

I say goodbye to the fears,

I say goodbye to the tears.

I say goodbye to the pain,

I say goodbye to the shame.

I say goodbye to the heartache,

I say goodbye to the bad days.

I say goodbye to the emotions,

I say goodbye to amber potions.

I say goodbye to the voices,

I say goodbye to the noises.

I say goodbye to the people,

I say goodbye to the needle.

With this toast I say goodbye.

I tearfully say goodbye to you,

I joyfully say goodbye to me.

Lie To Me

2 January 2018

Tell me that I am beautiful,

Even when I am not.

Tell me that I look alright,

Even when I do not.

Tell me that I am perfect,

Even though I am not.

Tell me that I am funny,

Even when I am not.

Tell me that I am paranoid,

Even when I am not.

Tell me that you still love me,

Even though you do not.

Tell me I am good enough,

Even though I am not.

Tell me that everything is okay,

Even when it is not.

Tell me that you don't see her,

Even when you do.

Tell me lies when I ask you,

Even though I know the truth.

save me

12 January 2018

Sunshine.
that's what you called me,
but it was Always a lie.
love.
that's what you said it was,
but it was never Verified.
Everything.
that's what i loved about you,
but My love was not enough.
broken.
that's how you left me.
how could i Ever be the same?

Ode to Rain

February 18 2018

The sky is so beautiful,

The sky is so gray.

The sky is cloudy,

Because it rained today.

The sky is so lovely,

The sky is not blue,

The sky is crying,

Because I don't have you.

The rain falls on my face,

And washes my tears away,

The rain gives me strength,

It helps me to be brave.

Now I am not lonely,

Because I have the rain.

Good Old Peter

6 February 2018

We'd been friends since childhood,
Good old Peter and me.
We did everything we ever could,
And took turns climbing up trees.
He told me I was his best friend,
That we would always be together.
Our summer days would never end,
Even in rainy weather.
But as good old Peter grew,
The less he came to visit.
He made more friends soon,
And didn't care how he did it.
He'd ignore me when he saw me,
And deny my existence.

It got to where he didn't look at me,
Even from a distance.
Good old Peter was no longer mine,
I realized this soon enough.
I decided to meet him one last time,
Before I left for good.
I went to him in the night,

When he was alone in his room.

That way he wouldn't have to hide,

And I wouldn't have to go so soon.

Good old Peter, he saw me there,

And he knew what was happening.

I sat down next to him, on his bed,

And I heard his heart singing.

He looked into my eyes

Then smiled a little smile.

He tried to apologize,

But I told him it was fine.

It was time for me to leave anyway,

Good old Peter was growing up.

And even though it broke my heart,

I let him go, and turned away.

After all, I'm only imaginary.

Who Am I?

4 April 2018

Who am I,

But a singer with no song?

Who am I?

But a road with no destination?

Who am I,

But a wind with no voice?

Who am I,

But an ocean with no depth?

Who am I,

But a lover with no heart?

Who am I,

But a leader with no virtue?

Who am I,

But a bird who cannot fly?

Who am I,

But a poet with no meaning?

Who am I,

But a clock with no hands?

Who am I,

But a heart with no emotion?

Who am I,

But a smile with no joy?

Who am I,

But a person with no purpose?

Who am I,

But a shameful fraud.

Colors

7 June 2018

Red,

My essence.

Orange,

The peace at dusk.

Yellow,

The happiness I feel.

Green,

The waves across the hills.

Blue,

The war within my soul.

Indigo,

The depths of curiosity.

Violet,

My inner prestige.

Black,

The end of life.

White,

The absence of colors.

Acknowledgements

I would like to thank everyone who read my poetry and gave me suggestions on how to perfect my technique. Writing poetry is quite difficult and I am grateful for all of the friends, family, and teachers who were there to keep me going. I wouldn't be able to write poetry without inspiration, and I would like to thank everyone who was the source of my inspiration. And finally, I wouldn't even have aspired to continue writing poetry if it weren't for my mother, who always makes sure I finish what I start. Thanks again to all of these wonderful people.

CPSIA information can be obtained
at www.ICGtesting.com
Printed in the USA
LVHW08s0747270718
585118LV00001BA/11/P